Paleo Slow Cooker

By

Tracy Daniels

Table of Contents

Introduction

The Paleolithic diet, often called the Paleo for short, is sometimes referred to as the caveman diet. Though it is a modern-day nutritional plan, this diet is based on the presumed dietary habits of early humans living during the Paleolithic era. It is said to be one of the healthiest diets in existence and the only diet to which humans are genetically adapted. In addition to being incredibly healthy, the Paleolithic diet has actually been documented to help control or reduce the risk of serious conditions such as heart disease and type 2 diabetes. This diet is particularly popular among people suffering from food sensitivities because it completely omits processed foods and focuses on simple cooking methods that preserve the natural integrity of food.

The Paleolithic diet first became popular during the 1970's when gastroenterologist Walter L. Voegtlin began to explore the concept of nutrition as it relates to evolutionary medicine. Voegtlin, along with several other authors and researchers, created the Paleolithic diet following the assumption that because human genetics have experienced little advancement over the course of time, modern humans must have the ability to thrive on the same diet followed by their ancestors. By returning to a more simplistic, natural approach to nutrition, Voegtlin believed it possible to cut out many of the harmful effects caused by modern dietary habits. Those who follow the Paleolithic diet are exposed to far fewer chemicals, preservatives and generally processed foods than the average consumer. These products are largely to blame for many diseases such as cardiovascular disease, high blood pressure and obesity which have reached epidemic levels in Western cultures.

The main principle of the Paleolithic diet is that only foods which can be hunted or gathered and eaten raw or with little preparation should be consumed. This means that any food that requires processing or refinement – foods like refined sugar, gluten grains, legumes, dairy products and fermented beverages are excluded from the Paleolithic diet. Proponents of the Paleolithic diet subsist largely on lean meat that is wild-caught or grass-fed, vegetables, fruit, fungi, roots and nuts. Some followers of the Paleolithic diet use alternatives to processed foods such as almond flour instead of wheat flour, coconut oil instead of butter and honey as a natural sweetener. There are some, however, who strictly adhere to the principles of the Paleolithic diet, consuming only raw foods.

As is true of any diet, the Paleolithic diet will take some time to get used to. For some people, it can be quite a challenge to eliminate processed foods from their diet and to begin focusing on healthier, more natural options. If you are up to the challenge, however, it will not be long before you begin to notice a difference in your body. Followers of the Paleolithic diet are likely to experience relief from food sensitivities and digestive issues as a result of returning to a more natural diet. Some people also experience improvement in athletic performance, weight loss and a general improvement in overall health. If you are serious about getting your body into the best shape possible and improving your health and longevity, the Paleolithic diet is the way to go.

Though many benefits of the Paleolithic diet are indisputable, some potential followers of the diet experience concern over the challenges of this type of nutritional plan. Many people believe that healthy, natural foods are very expensive and thus stock their pantries with inexpensive, processed foods. In reality, healthy organic foods can be just as affordable as processed foods if you know how to shop. Another common concern related to the Paleolithic diet is that many people simply do not know how to prepare fresh foods correctly. The truth of the matter is that preparing healthy foods can be as simple as you want it to be. There are countless Paleo recipes out there that take minutes to prepare and you do not even need any special tools or equipment. In fact, you can make a variety of Paleolithic diet-friendly meals using your slow cooker. If you are looking for a way to ease yourself into the Paleolithic diet, these slow cooker recipes are a great way to go. Not only are they all simple to prepare, but they are healthy and delicious as well. Whether you are a longtime follower of the Paleolithic diet or just getting started, these slow cooker recipes will make a wonderful addition to your recipe repertoire.

Soups and Stews

Whether you are cooking for you entire family or just for yourself, slow cooker soups and stews are a simple way to make a dish that lasts. Depending on the size of your slow cooker, you can adjust the size of these recipes to make more for a large family gathering or dinner party – you can also decrease the size of the recipe or freeze some of it if you are cooking for just one or two. These Paleo soups and stews utilize fresh, flavorful ingredients so you do not need a lot of seasoning. If you have your own herb garden, however, or have access to fresh organic herbs, don't be afraid to experiment by adding some of your own flavoring to these recipes. By using a little bit of creativity you can customize these slow cooker recipes to create something your entire family will love.

Cashew Chicken Soup

Inspired by a West African dish, this recipe for cashew chicken soup may be something you've never tried before. Despite being out of the ordinary, peanut chicken soup is a delicious, low-carb recipe that is perfectly suited to the Paleolithic diet. If you want to make your soup a little more substantial, feel free to add more vegetables such as squash, beans or kale.

Number of Servings: 5   **Prep Time:** 30 minutes

Ingredients:

1 medium onion, sliced thin
4 cloves garlic, minced
1 tsp. ground ginger
12 oz. chicken breast, cubed
6 cups chicken broth
1 can diced tomatoes
2 cups zucchini, cut into chunks
½ cup smooth peanut butter
Salt and pepper to taste
1 oz. dry roasted cashews for garnish

Instructions:

1. Place the cubed chicken in the slow cooker and sprinkle the sliced onions on top.
2. Add the minced garlic and dried ginger.
3. Pour in about 5 ½ cups of chicken broth and turn the heat on HIGH for 1 hour.
4. Reduce the heat to LOW and stir in the diced tomatoes and zucchini.
5. Combine the remaining ½ cup of chicken broth with the peanut butter and add it to the slow cooker, stirring to incorporate it.
6. Cook on LOW for 4 to 6 hours until the zucchini is tender and the chicken is cooked through.
7. Season with salt and pepper to taste then garnish with dry roasted cashews and serve.

Nutritional Information:
345 calories, 68 calories from fat, 27 g protein, 16 g carbohydrates, 17 g fat, 9 g sugar

Roasted Leek, Potato and Onion Soup

There is some debate as to whether potatoes are truly part of the Paleolithic diet but, for the most part, it is up to the individual to decide whether to include them in this recipe or not. If you choose to omit the potatoes, you can simply add another leek and an extra onion to the existing list of ingredients. Without the potatoes, however, you should be aware that the soup will retain more of a broth-like consistency – it will not be as thick and creamy as it would be with the potatoes.

Number of Servings: 6   **Prep Time:** 30 minutes

Ingredients:

2 lbs. Yukon gold potatoes, peeled and diced
5 cups chicken stock
2 leeks, rinsed and chops (white and light green parts only)
1 onion, chopped
3 cloves garlic, minced
1 cup coconut milk
Salt and pepper to taste

Instructions:

1. Dice the potatoes into 1-inch chunks and chop the leeks and onion.
2. Add all the vegetables to the slow cooker and sprinkle the minced garlic on top.

3. Pour the chicken stock over the ingredients in the slow cooker then cover and heat on Low heat for 7 to 8 hours or until the potatoes are tender.
4. Turn off the slow cooker and blend the soup using an immersion blender, if desired.
5. Stir in the coconut milk and season with salt and pepper to taste. Serve hot.

Nutritional Information:

163 calories, 9 calories from fat, 6 g protein, 35 g carbohydrates, 1 g fat, 4 g sugar

Cooking Tips: If you prefer to leave your soup chunky, you can skip step 4. If you want your soup to be creamy but do not have an immersion blender, try pureeing the soup in batches in the blender.

Chicken and Sweet Potato Stew

If you are looking for a recipe to warm you up on a cool Autumn or Winter evening, try this recipe for chicken and sweet potato stew. This recipe is the perfect combination of protein and vegetables – you get the protein from the chicken as well as the nutrients and subtly sweet flavor from the sweet potato. For a lighter meal, try making this recipe without the chicken and puree it in the blender for a delicious, creamy sweet potato soup.

Number of Servings: 6   **Prep Time:** 20 minutes

Ingredients:

3 lbs. boneless skinless chicken breasts, cubed

3 small sweet potatoes, chopped

1 onion, chopped

3 carrots, sliced on the bias

1 stalk celery, sliced on the bias

2 cups water

Salt and pepper to taste

Instructions:

1. Trim the fat from the chicken breasts and cut them into 1-inch cubes. Add the cubed chicken to the slow cooker.
2. Add the chopped sweet potatoes, onion, carrots and celery to the slow cooker.

13

3. Pour the water into the slow cooker then cover and heat on Low heat for 6 to 8 hours or until the chicken is cooked through.
4. Season with salt and pepper to taste. Serve hot.

Nutritional Information:

320calories, 27 calories from fat, 52 g protein, 19 g carbohydrates, 3 g fat, 7 g sugar

Tomato Basil Soup

No matter what diet you follow, tomato basil soup is a well-loved classic. Not only is this recipe incredibly simple to prepare, but the addition of fresh basil gives it a flavor that is difficult to top. If you keep your own garden during the summer, this is the perfect way to use some of your homegrown produce. Even if you don't grow your own produce it is a great way to take advantage of summer farm stands and farmers markets.

Number of Servings: 4   **Prep Time:** 15 minutes

Ingredients:

10 large tomatoes, cored and cut in half
1 large onion, sliced
3 cloves garlic, minced
2 tbsp. olive oil
1 cup water
6 to 8 leaves fresh basil, chopped
½ cup coconut milk
Salt and pepper to taste

Instructions:

1. Arrange the halved tomatoes in the bottom of the slow cooker and sprinkle the sliced onions and minced garlic on top.
2. Drizzle the olive oil over the ingredients in the slow cooker then cover and cook on High heat for one hour or until the tomatoes are tender.
3. Add the water and fresh basil to the slow cooker then cover and cook on Low heat for 4 to 6 hours.
4. Turn off the slow cooker and blend the soup using an immersion blender or by pureeing it in batches using a blender.
5. Stir in the coconut milk, season to taste with salt and pepper then serve hot.

Nutritional Information:

172 calories, 64 calories from fat, 5 g protein, 24 g carbohydrates, 9 g fat, 14 g sugar

Cooking Tips: You may also use canned whole tomatoes for this recipe but, in order to stay within the guidelines of the Paleolithic diet, be sure to use a brand that doesn't use BPA in the lining of their cans. You may even be able to find jarred organic tomatoes in order to avoid can-related problems entirely.

Greek Stew

Made with braised beef, this recipe for slow cooker Greek stew is the perfect way to warm up on a cold winter night. If you are tired of using the same old recipes, give this recipe a try. Not only will the unique flavor of braised beef satisfy your taste buds but it blends perfectly with tender onions and the flavor of bay leaves to create a unique and healthy dish.

Number of Servings: 8   **Prep Time:** 30 minutes

Ingredients:

3 lbs. grass-fed beef, cubed
3 tbsp. coconut oil
1 onion, chopped
10 cloves garlic, minced
1 cup diced tomatoes
½ cup water
2 bay leaves
Salt and pepper to taste

Instructions:

1. Heat the coconut oil in a skillet over medium high heat. Add the cubed beef and cook until it is browned on all sides, 3 to 5 minutes.

2. Spoon the meat out of the skillet and into the slow cooker. Pour the juices into a small bowl and set aside.
3. Add the chopped onion and minced garlic to the skillet and cook over medium high heat until translucent.
4. Sprinkle the cooked onions and garlic over the beef in the slow cooker then drizzle with the meat juice. Add the diced tomatoes, bay leaf and water.
5. Cover and cook on HIGH heat for 4 hours.
6. Season with salt and pepper to taste.

Nutritional Information:

404 calories, 189 calories from fat, 46 g protein, 5 g carbohydrates, 21 g fat, 1 g sugar

Cooking Tips: When cooking with bay leaf, always remove the bay leaf before serving the dish. To make this dish more substantial, feel free to add some Yukon gold potatoes cut into large chunks.

Jambalaya Soup

Jambalaya is a classic New Orleans-style dish which can be made using a variety of ingredients. Though traditional Jambalaya is made with rice, you can substitute cauliflower rice and still enjoy the flavors of this delicious, Paleolithic diet-friendly dish. If you are a fan of spicy food, feel free to add more hot sauce or a dash of cayenne to kick this recipe up a notch.

Number of Servings: 6   **Prep Time:** 15 minutes

Ingredients:

5 cups chicken broth
3 bell peppers, chopped
1 can organic diced tomatoes
1 medium onion, chopped
2 cloves garlic, minced
1lb raw shrimp, peeled and deveined
1/3lb chicken, cubed
1lb spicy chicken sausage, sliced
1/2 head cauliflower
1 tsp. paprika
1 tsp. salt
1 tsp. garlic powder
½ tsp. black pepper
½ tsp. dried oregano
½ tsp. dried thyme
½ tsp. onion powder

½ tsp. cayenne pepper

Instructions:

1. Place the chicken, chopped peppers, onion and garlic in the slow cooker. Sprinkle the spices on top and drizzle with chicken stock.
2. Cover and cook on LOW heat for 5 hours until the chicken is cooked through.
3. Add the sliced sausage and cook for an additional 30 minutes.
4. Cut up the cauliflower into large chunks and pulse it in a food processer to create a cauliflower rice.
5. Add the cauliflower rice and shrimp to the slow cooker and cook for 20 minutes.
6. Garnish with sliced scallions and serve hot.

Nutritional Information:
281 calories, 72 calories from fat, 37 g protein, 14 g carbohydrates, 8 g fat, 6 g sugar

Cooking Tips: If you prefer the presentation of traditional jambalaya over this soup version, try reducing the amount of chicken broth suggested by the recipe to 1 cup and serve the jambalaya over steamed cauliflower rice rather than adding the rice to the slow cooker.

Butternut Squash Soup

Butternut squash soup is a classic fall favorite and by using your slow cooker, it is also incredibly easy to make. Whether you are looking for a delicious dish to serve your family or something nice to serve at a dinner party, this recipe for slow cooker butternut squash soup is sure to please. If you have access to a local farmer's market or are able to grow the squash yourself, your soup will be both healthy and natural – a great example of a Paleolithic diet meal.

Number of Servings: 6   **Prep Time:** 20 minutes

Ingredients:

2 butternut squashes
1 can coconut milk
1 onion, chopped
3 cups vegetable broth
½ tsp. dried marjoram
Salt and pepper to taste

Instructions:

1. Cut the butternut squashes in half and scoop out the center. Peel the squash and cut it into cubes.
2. Place the squash cubes and chopped onion in the slow cooker and add the vegetable broth and dried marjoram.

3. Cover and cook on LOW heat for 6 to 8 hours.
4. Use an immersion blender to puree the soup then stir in the coconut milk.
5. Season with salt and pepper to taste. Serve hot.

Nutritional Information:

71 calories, 9 calories from fat, 1 g protein, 15 g carbohydrates, 1 g fat, 5 g sugar

Cooking Tips: If you do not have an immersion blender you can either puree the soup in batches in your blender or use a potato masher to puree the squash by hand. If you mash the squash by hand your soup may not be creamy, but it will be easier to blend in the coconut milk than if you did not mash the squash at all.

Thai Curry Chicken Soup

Just because you have chosen to follow the Paleolithic diet doesn't mean you have to give up some of your favorite ethnic foods. There are plenty of ways to create your own Thai favorites from scratch while still sticking to your diet! Not only is this recipe for Thai curry chicken soup delicious, but because you can make it in the slow cooker it takes no time at all to prepare.

Number of Servings: 6   **Prep Time:** 10 minutes

Ingredients:

½ lb. chicken breast, chopped

1 onion, diced

2 bell peppers, chopped

1 cup sliced mushrooms

2 cups chicken stock

3 cups coconut milk

3 tbsp. curry powder

Salt and pepper to taste

Instructions:

1. Place the cubed chicken in the slow cooker then add the onion, peppers and mushrooms.
2. Pour the chicken stock over the vegetables in the slow cooker and stir in the curry powder.
3. Cover and cook on LOW heat for 4 to 6 hours until the chicken is cooked through and the vegetables are tender.

4. Stir in the coconut milk to thicken the soup.
5. Garnish with fresh cilantro and serve hot.

Nutritional Information:

114 calories, 36 calories from fat, 11g protein, 10 g carbohydrates, 4 g fat, 5 g sugar

Cooking Tips: If you prefer a thicker curry, try stirring a tablespoon of almond flour into the chicken stock before adding it to the slow cooker. As the soup cooks, the flour will help to thicken it.

Poultry

Some proponents of the Paleolithic diet try to mimic the diet of our Paleolithic ancestors down to the plant-to-animal food ratio. Though there is some debate about the perfect ratio, most researchers suggest that hunter-gatherer societies subsist on a diet that is composed of 64% to 68% calories from animal sources and the remaining 32% to 36% from plant sources. Protein plays a very important role in the Paleolithic diet and poultry sources such as chicken and turkey are very high in protein. When selecting poultry for use in Paleolithic diet recipes look for lean cuts of chicken or turkey that comes from free-range birds. If possible, stick to white-meat, skinless breasts to receive the optimal nutritional value with the least amount of fat.

Lemon Garlic Chicken

By using a whole roasting chicken in this recipe, you can greatly cut down on the preparation time. If, however, you prefer to use a leaner cut of chicken such as boneless skinless breasts, you can substitute a different cut of chicken at the same weight. This recipe is simple to prepare but full of flavor – it pairs well with fresh, seasonal veggies and you can season it with whatever herbs you have on hand.

Number of Servings: 6   **Prep Time:** 10 Minutes

Ingredients:

1 whole roasting chicken (3 to 5 lbs.)
30 cloves garlic, peeled
1 onion, sliced
1 lemon
½ tsp. dried thyme
½ tsp. dried rosemary
1 tsp. Italian seasoning
Salt and pepper to taste

Instructions:

1. Place the sliced onions and peeled garlic in the bottom of the slow cooker.
2. Rinse the chicken and pat it dry then add it to the slow cooker on top of the garlic and onions.
3. Juice the lemon and pour the juice over the chicken then place the lemon halves inside the cavity of the chicken.

4. Season the chicken with the spices then cover and cook on LOW heat for 5 to 6 hours until the chicken reaches an internal temperature of 165°F.
5. Remove the chicken from the slow cooker and cover with foil. Let sit for 15 minutes before carving.
6. Serve hot with cooked garlic and onions for garnish.

Nutritional Information:

424 calories, 243 calories from fat, 38 g protein, 7 g carbohydrates, 27 g fat, 1 g sugar

Lettuce Wrapped Chicken

This slow cooker recipe for Paleo chicken lettuc wraps is the perfect appetizer for any dinner party or family get together. The Asian-style sauce flavors the chicken beautifully while the slow cooker keeps it moist and tender. Don't be afraid to customize this recipe using a different sauce or by adding ingredients like bean sprouts or additional vegetables!

Number of Servings: 6   **Prep Time:** 15 minutes

Ingredients:

2 lbs. boneless skinless chicken breast, chopped

4 tbsp. coconut aminos

2 tbsp. almond butter

1 tbsp. pure honey

2 tbsp. vinegar

3 cloves garlic, minced

Salt and pepper to taste

Leaf lettuce

Instructions:

1. Place the chopped chicken in the slow cooker.
2. Combine the remaining ingredients except for the lettuce in a small bowl and whisk to combine.
3. Pour the sauce over the chicken in the slow cooker.
4. Cover and cook on LOW heat for 4 to 6 hours until the chicken is cooked through.

5. Serve hot with large pieces of lettuce for wrapping.

Nutritional Information:

216 calories, 36 calories from fat, 37 g protein, 6 g carbohydrates, 4 g fat, 5 g sugar

Cooking Tips: Coconut aminos are derived from the sap of the coconut flower and this sauce is a widely accepted Paleo-friendly alternative to soy sauce. While soy-based sauces contain a small amount of healthy amino acids, coconut aminos is abundant in amino acids, vitamins and minerals.

Turkey and Gravy

A fresh twist on a well-loved classic, this recipe for turkey and gravy is just what you need to warm you up on a cold winter night. The best part of this recipe is that you can customize it with your favorite herbs and spices to give the gravy that homemade flavor. There are a variety of ways to serve this dish – serve it over a bed of steamed veggies if you like or, if you include grains in your diet in moderation, on a bed of whole wheat noodles or brown rice.

Number of Servings: 6   **Prep Time:**

Ingredients:

4lb boneless turkey breasts
2 tbsp. olive oil
2 onions, chopped
6 cloves garlic, minced
1 tsp. tomato paste
¼ cup chicken stock
Salt and pepper to taste

Instructions:

1. Heat the olive oil in a large skillet over medium high heat. Add the turkey breasts and cook until browned on both sides, about 5 minutes.
2. Remove the turkey and place it in the slow cooker.

3. Add the onions and garlic to the skillet, cooking until translucent then add them to the slow cooker.
4. Whisk together the tomato paste and chicken stock then add it to the skillet. Cook over medium heat, whisking occasionally until it begins to thicken. Season with salt and pepper to taste.
5. Pour the gravy over the turkey in the slow cooker.
6. Cover and cook on LOW heat for 6 to 8 hours until turkey is cooked through.
7. Use two forks to shred the turkey then serve hot.

Nutritional Information:

453 calories, 135 calories from fat, 68 g protein, 5 g carbohydrates, 15 g fat, 2 g sugar

Teriyaki Chicken Drumsticks

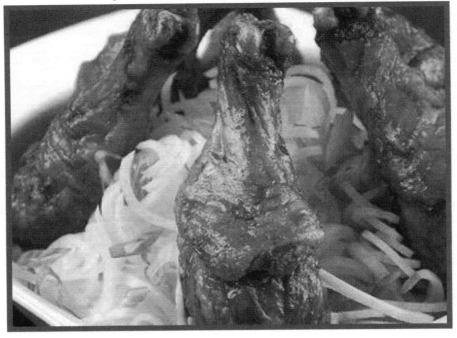

Number of Servings: 4   **Prep Time:** 10 Minutes

Ingredients:

1lb chicken drumsticks, skin removed
½ cup coconut aminos
1 cup pineapple, diced
¼ tsp. garlic powder
¾ tsp. ground ginger
1 tbsp. olive oil

Instructions:

1. Place the chicken drumsticks in the slow cooker and add the diced pineapple.
2. Combine the coconut aminos, garlic powder, ground ginger and olive oil in a small bowl then drizzle over the ingredients in the slow cooker.
3. Cover and cook on LOW heat for 6 to 8 hours or on HIGH for 3 to 4 hours until chicken is cooked through.
4. Serve hot on a bed of bean sprouts.

Nutritional Information:
198 calories, 63 calories from fat, 28 g protein, 8 g carbohydrates, 7 g fat, 4 g sugar

Asparagus Chicken Roll-Ups

If you are looking for a unique but healthy recipe to serve at your next dinner party, try out these asparagus chicken roll-ups. The tenderness of the chicken pairs perfectly with the crunch of fresh asparagus and the creaminess of feta cheese. If you prefer not to include dairy in your diet, feel free to omit the feta cheese from this recipe or replace it with some chopped onion to enhance the flavor of these chicken roll-ups.

Number of Servings: 5   **Prep Time:** 30 minutes

Ingredients:

4 boneless skinless chicken breasts
1 bunch asparagus
2 cloves garlic, minced
Salt and pepper to taste

Instructions:

1. Filet the chicken breasts then lay them out flat. Use a meat mallet to pound the chicken breast filets to a thickness of approximately ¼ to ½ inch.
2. Cut the asparagus in half so it is equal in length to the width of your chicken breast fillets.
3. Lay one piece of asparagus in the center of each chicken breast fillet.
4. Sprinkle some minced garlic on top of the asparagus then roll up the fillets and secure them with wooden toothpicks.
5. Season the roll-ups with salt and pepper then place in the slow cooker.

6. Cover and cook on LOW heat for 4 hours until chicken is cooked through.

Nutritional Information:

202 calories, 45 calories from fat, 36 g protein, 2 g carbohydrates, 5 g fat, 1 g sugar

Spicy Pulled Chicken

Number of Servings: 6   **Prep Time:** 10 Minutes

Ingredients:

4 boneless, skinless chicken breasts

1 red pepper, diced

1 onion, diced

1 tbsp. olive oil

1 cup chicken broth

1 tsp. cayenne pepper

1 tsp. chili powder

Salt and pepper to taste

Instructions:

1. Place the chicken breasts in the slow cooker.
2. Add the diced onion and red pepper on top of the chicken breasts.
3. Drizzle the olive oil over the ingredients in the slow cooker.
4. Combine the chicken broth, cayenne, chili powder, salt and pepper then drizzle over the ingredients in the slow cooker.
5. Cover and cook on LOW heat for 6 to 8 hours or on HIGH for 3 to 4 hours until chicken is cooked through.
6. Use two forks to shred the chicken then stir in the onions and peppers before serving.

Nutritional Information:

200 calories, 36 calories from fat, 18 g protein, 4 g carbohydrates, 4 g fat, 3 g sugar

Cooking Tips: This spicy pulled chicken can be served a variety of ways. Try serving it in a lettuce wrap for a quick and tasty lunch or mix in some steamed vegetables to make it a complete meal.

Turkey and Cabbage

If you are looking for a light, healthy lunch option this recipe for slow cooker turkey and cabbage may be just the thing. The perfect combination of protein and veggies, turkey and cabbage is a simple yet delicious recipe. Don't be afraid to add more cabbage if you like or, if you have a garden at home, throw in some extra veggies!

Number of Servings: 4   **Prep Time:** 15 Minutes

Ingredients:

4 boneless turkey breasts, cubed

1 onion, chopped

4 carrots, sliced on the bias

½ head cabbage, sliced

2 cups chicken broth

1 tsp. salt

½ tsp. pepper

Instructions:

1. Place the onions, carrots and cabbage in the slow cooker.
2. Combine the chicken broth, salt and pepper in a small bowl. Drizzle half the mixture over the ingredients in the slow cooker.
3. Add the turkey breasts on top of the vegetables and pour on the remaining broth mixture.

4. Cover and cook on LOW for 6 to 7 hours or on HIGH heat for 3 to 4 hours until turkey is cooked through.

Nutritional Information:

276 calories, 18 calories from fat, 52 g protein, 18 g carbohydrates, 2 g fat, 10 g sugar

Chicken Cacciatore

Chicken cacciatore is a classic italian recipe that is typically prepared "hunter" style with fresh tomatoes, onions and herbs. This natural preparation style makes it the perfect recipe for the Paleolithic diet, especially if you are looking for something easy to prepare that has a lot of flavor. Not only can you prepare this recipe in ten minutes or less, but by using your slow cooker you can turn it on when you leave for work in the morning and come home to a meal that is ready to enjoy.

Number of Servings: 4   **Prep Time:** 10 Minutes

Ingredients:

1lb chicken legs
1 onion, sliced thin
3 bell peppers, sliced
1 stalk celery, sliced on the bias
1 cup tomatoes, diced
2 cloves garlic, minced
3 tbsp. olive oil
Salt and pepper to taste

Instructions:

1. Place the chicken in the slow cooker and sprinkle the onions, peppers, celery and garlic on top.

2. Drizzle the olive oil over the ingredients in the slow cooker and season to taste with salt and pepper.
3. Add the chopped tomatoes then cover and cook on LOW heat for 8 hours or until the chicken is cooked through and the vegetables are tender.
4. Garnish with fresh parsley and serve hot.

Nutritional Information:

349 calories, 261 calories from fat, 14 g protein, 10 g carbohydrates, 29 g fat, 6 g sugar

Cooking Tips: Though typically served on a bed of noodles, your Paleo chicken cacciatore can be served up on a plate of steamed spinach or by itself in a bowl. If you do not strictly follow the Paleolithic diet and allow yourself to consume some grain, this recipe can also be served on a bed of brown rice.

Beef and Lamb

Grass-fed beef and lamb are two staples of the Paleolithic diet. Not only are these foods high in protein, but they are also rich in a variety of other nutrients that your body needs to stay healthy. When selecting cuts of beef and lamb to use in these recipes, look for leaner cuts or trim away the excess fat yourself. Doing so will help you to limit your fat intake while still benefiting from the high protein content of beef and lamb dishes. From traditional stews and casseroles to unique dishes like Osso Buco, the options are virtually limitless when you combine your slow cooker with a good cut of beef or lamb.

BBQ Short Ribs

You don't have to spend hours standing next to a hot grill just to enjoy some barbecue short ribs. By making your own barbecue sauce and utilizing your slow cooker you can create a batch of flavorful, Paleolithic diet-friendly beef ribs with little effort at all. Simply load up your slow cooker and let it do its work – when you return a few hours later, you will have a pot full of savory, fall-of-the-bone ribs.

Number of Servings: 8   **Prep Time:** 15 minutes

Ingredients:

3lb grass-fed short ribs
2 onions, sliced
¾ cup tomato paste
½ cup apple cider vinegar
½ cup water
1 tbsp. coconut aminos
3 tbsp. mustard powder
1 tbsp. organic honey
Salt and pepper to taste

Instructions:

1. Place the sliced onions in the bottom of the slow cooker and add the short ribs.
2. Whisk together the remaining ingredients to create the bbq sauce then pour over the ingredients in the slow cooker.
3. Cover and cook on LOW heat for 6 to 8 hours until the beef is tender.

Nutritional Information:

468 calories, 342 calories from fat, 21 g protein, 9 g carbohydrates, 38 g fat, 6 g sugar

Spicy Beef Stew

Beef stew is a very traditional dish but you can add a little bit of flair to it by adding some chili powder and cayenne pepper. Try out this recipe at your next dinner party and watch your guests' faces light up in surprise and delight as they take the first bite of what they assume to be traditional beef stew.

Number of Servings: 4   **Prep Time:** 15 Minutes

Ingredients:

1 ½ lbs. stew beef
2 tsp. coconut oil
1 large onion, quartered
2 carrots, sliced
1 can organic diced tomatoes
1/2 cup beef broth
2 tsp. chili powder
2 tsp. garlic powder
½ tsp. cayenne
Salt and pepper to taste

Instructions:

1. Heat the coconut oil in a large skillet over medium heat. Add the stew beef and cook until brown in all sides, about five minutes.
2. Add the beef, onions, carrots and diced tomatoes to the slow cooker.
3. Whisk together the beef broth and spices then add to the slow cooker.
4. Cover and cook on HIGH heat for 3 to 4 hours or on LOW for 6 to 8 hours until beef is tender.

Nutritional Information:

359 calories, 162 calories from fat, 33 g protein, 12 g carbohydrates, 18 g fat, 7 g sugar

Sweet Balsamic Roast Beef

Roast beef is often considered a fancy meal for special occasions but by using your slow cooker you can turn it into an everyday meal! Simply load up your slow cooker with the roast along with some of your favorite vegetables like sweet onions to add some flavor. Next, drizzle on a little balsamic vinegar and some of your favorite spices then turn on the slow cooker and walk away. It is as simple as that!

Number of Servings: 6   **Prep Time:** 10 Minutes

Ingredients:

2lb beef roast
1 large Vidalia onion, sliced
1 cup organic tomato sauce
½ cup water
½ cup balsamic vinegar
1 tbsp. organic honey
1 tbsp. coconut oil
Salt and pepper to taste

Instructions:

1. Season the roast with salt and pepper.
2. Heat the coconut oil in a large skillet over medium heat. Add the roast and cook for 2 to 3 minutes on each side until browned.
3. Add the onions to the slow cooker then place the browned roast on top.
4. Whisk together the tomato sauce, water, balsamic vinegar and honey then pour over the roast.

46

5. Cover and cook on LOW heat for 6 to 8 hours or on HIGH heat for 5 to 6 hours until beef is tender.

Nutritional Information:

292 calories, 126 calories from fat, 30 g protein, 13 g carbohydrates, 14 g fat, 8 g sugar

Meatloaf

Meatloaf is a timeless classic and it is one that can easily be adapted to the slow cooker. After combining the ingredients and forming your loaf, all you have to do is put it in the slow cooker and let the appliance do the rest of the work. You should be aware, however, that as the meatloaf cooks some of the fat will drain out of it so it is best to raise the meatloaf on a slow cooker insert rack or lay down a bed of crumpled foil.

Number of Servings: 6   **Prep Time:** 10 Minutes

Ingredients:

1lb lean ground beef
1lb ground lamb
1 medium onion, diced
1 bell pepper, diced
1 egg, beaten
¼ tsp. garlic powder
Salt and pepper to taste

Instructions:

1. Combine all ingredients in a large bowl, mixing by hand until well blended.
2. Place a rack or a layer of crumpled foil in the bottom of the slow cooker to keep the meatloaf out of the fat as it cooks.
3. Place the meatloaf in the slow cooker.

4. Cover and cook on HIGH heat for 4 to 6 hours until the loaf is cooked through.
5. Cool slightly then remove from slow cooker and slice to serve.

Nutritional Information:

389 calories, 243 calories from fat, 33 g protein, 3 g carbohydrates, 27 g fat, 2 g sugar

Beef with Broccoli

Normally a popular Chinese food dish, beef with broccoli can easily be made at home in your slow cooker. The perfect combination of protein and vegetables, beef with broccoli is a great choice for either lunch or dinner. Take advantage of the fresh produce at your local farmers market and don't be afraid to make additions to the recipe – try adding some fresh carrots or onions to enhance the flavor of this dish.

Number of Servings: 4   **Prep Time:** 15 Minutes

Ingredients:

2lbs stew meat
2 heads broccoli
4 cloves garlic, minced
1 onion, chopped
1/3 cup coconut aminos
1 cup organic beef stock
½ tsp. ground ginger
Salt and pepper to taste

Instructions:

1. Place the stew meat, garlic and onion in the slow cooker.
2. Whisk together the coconut aminos, beef stock, ginger, salt and pepper then pour over the ingredients in the slow cooker.
3. Cover and cook on LOW heat for 5 to 6 hours.
4. Cut the broccoli into florets and add to the slow cooker.

50

5. Cover again and cook on LOW heat for an additional 1 to 2 hours until broccoli is tender and beef is cooked through.

Nutritional Information:

446 calories, 180 calories from fat, 45 g protein, 5 g carbohydrates, 20 g fat, 1 g sugar

Easy Lamb Roast

You may be one of many people who are under the impression that roasting lamb is a difficult process that takes hours to complete. While it may be true that cooking a lamb roast can take hours, the preparation process can actually be very simple if you choose to use your slow cooker. Once you have prepared the ingredients and loaded them into your slow cooker all you have to do is wait and enjoy the delicious aromas that begin to fill your house.

Number of Servings: 5   **Prep Time:** 10 Minutes

Ingredients:

2 ½ lbs. lamb roast, bone in
6 cloves garlic, peeled and sliced
1 large onion, sliced
1 sprig fresh rosemary
1 cup water
Salt and pepper to taste

Instructions:

1. Place the lamb roast in the middle of the slow cooker.
2. Sprinkle the garlic, onions salt and pepper over the roast.
3. Pour the water into the bottom of the slow cooker and place the sprig of rosemary on top of the roast.
4. Cover and cook on LOW heat for 7 to 8 hours until lamb is cooked through.

Nutritional Information:

360 calories,153 calories from fat, 44g protein,4 g carbohydrates, 17 g fat, 1 g sugar

Lamb Curry

Lamb curry is a wonderful meal to serve your family on a cold winter night. The spice of the lamb will wake up your taste buds while the sweet potatoes provide a perfect balance. Serve this dish over a bed of riced cauliflower or spaghetti squash to make it a complete meal.

Number of Servings: 6   **Prep Time:** 15 Minutes

Ingredients:

2lb boneless lamb shoulder

2 tbsp. olive oil

1 onion, chopped

3 cloves garlic, minced

1 (10 oz.) can diced organic tomatoes

4 medium sweet potatoes

1 cup water

1 tbsp. curry powder

2 tsp. cumin

¼ tsp. turmeric

1/8 tsp. cayenne

Salt and pepper to taste

Fresh cilantro

Instructions:

1. Season the lamb shoulder with salt and pepper to taste.
2. Heat the olive oil in a large skillet over medium heat. Add the lamb shoulder and cook for 2 to 3 minutes on each side or until browned.
3. Add the onions, garlic and diced tomatoes to the slow cooker.
4. Place the browned lamb in the slow cooker on top of the vegetables.
5. Whisk together the water, curry powder, cumin and turmeric. Pour over the ingredients in the slow cooker.
6. Cover and cook on LOW heat for 4 hours or until the lamb is tender.
7. Remove the lamb from the slow cooker and place it on a cutting board.
8. Add the chopped sweet potatoes then cover and cook on LOW heat for an additional hour.
9. Shred the lamb with a fork while the sweet potatoes are cooking then add it back to the slow cooker and cook it on LOW for another 10 minutes to warm it up.
10. Serve hot and garnish with fresh cilantro.

Nutritional Information:

651 calories, 378 calories from fat, 44 g protein, 23 g carbohydrates, 42 g fat, 10 g sugar

Lamb Stew

Lamb stew is a simple winter time favorite that is both delicious and easy to make. If you want to come home from work to a hot meal already waiting for you, don't hesitate to try this recipe! While most traditional stews use beef, lamb is actually just as flavorful and easy to use. Don't be afraid to add more vegetables or to swap out those called for in the recipe – get creative and customize this dish to suit your tastes!

Number of Servings: 6   **Prep Time:** 15 Minutes

Ingredients:

3lb bone-in lamb shank
2 tbsp. olive oil
1 large onion, chopped
3 large carrots, sliced
2 cups cabbage, chopped
3 sweet potatoes, diced
1 cup water
1 sprig fresh rosemary
Salt and pepper to taste

Instructions:

1. Season the lamb shank with salt and pepper to taste.

2. Heat the olive oil in a large skillet over medium heat. Add the lamb shank and cook for 2 to 3 minutes on each side or until browned.
3. Add the onions, carrots and cabbage to the slow cooker.
4. Place the browned lamb in the slow cooker on top of the vegetables.
5. Pour the water over the ingredients in the slow cooker and place the sprig of rosemary on top of the lamb.
6. Cover and cook on LOW heat for 6 to 8 hours until the lamb is tender.
7. Dice the sweet potatoes and add them to the slow cooker during the last hour of cooking.
8. Serve hot and garnish with fresh parsley.

Nutritional Information:

656 calories, 387 calories from fat, 43 g protein, 24 g carbohydrates, 43 g fat, 11 g sugar

Dried Apricot Lamb Casserole

Lamb and dried apricots may sound like a strange combination to you but the subtle sweetness of the apricots pairs nicely with the salty, savoryness of the lamb in this casserole. Try out this dish at your next dinner party and you may be surprised to find that your guests love this dried apricot lamb casserole so much that it becomes the main topic of discussion for the evening!

Number of Servings: 6   **Prep Time:** 15 Minutes

Ingredients:

2lbs lamb, cubed

2 tsp. coconut oil

1 onion, chopped

3 cloves garlic, minced

2 cups tomatoes, diced

2 cups dried apricots, quartered

1 tsp. ground cinnamon

1 tsp. ground cumin

Salt and pepper to taste

Instructions:

1. Combine the lamb, coconut oil, cinnamon, cumin, salt and pepper in a medium bowl and mix thoroughly to coat the lamb with the spices.
2. Heat a large skillet over medium heat and add the lamb. Stir the meat until it browns evenly.

3. Remove the lamb from the skillet and place it in the slow cooker. Pour a small amount of water into the skillet to loosen the browned bits on the bottom then add the liquid to the slow cooker.
4. Add the onion, garlic, diced tomatoes and dried apricots to the slow cooker.
5. Cover and cook on LOW heat for 6 to 8 hours until the lamb is tender.
6. Serve hot on a bed of spaghetti squash or riced cauliflower.

Nutritional Information:

371 calories, 90 calories from fat, 33 g protein, 39 g carbohydrates, 10 g fat, 32 g sugar

Osso Buco with Garlic Marinara

If you are looking for a unique, flavorful recipe to serve your family and friends you have come to the right place. This recipe for Osso Buco with garlic marinara is sure to please and surprise your guests. If you have never cooked osso buco before, you are missing out on a world of wonderful flavors.

Number of Servings: 5   **Prep Time:** 15 Minutes

Ingredients:

3 lb. cross-cut beef shanks with marrow bones

1 tbsp. olive oil

1 onion, diced

1 can roasted diced tomatoes

2 cups organic tomato sauce

6 cloves garlic, minced

1 cup organic beef broth

1 tbsp. dried basil

1 tsp. oregano

Salt and pepper to taste

Instructions:

1. Heat the olive oil in a large skillet over medium heat. Add the beef shanks, season them with salt and pepper then cook for 2 to 3 minutes on each side until browned.
2. Place the beef shanks in the slow cooker.

3. Add the onion, diced tomatoes, tomato sauce and garlic to the slow cooker.
4. Whisk together the beef broth, dried basil and oregano. Drizzle over the ingredients in the slow cooker.
5. Cover and cook on LOW heat for 7 to 8 hours.
6. Serve hot with freshly steamed vegetables.

Nutritional Information:

442 calories, 117 calories from fat, 61 g protein, 16 g carbohydrates, 13 g fat, 5 g sugar

Fish and Seafood

When it comes to cooking seafood, you have probably never thought to use your slow cooker. Traditional cooking methods for fish and seafood typically include baking, frying and grilling but a slow cooker is another great option. The key to cooking seafood in the slow cooker is to avoid overcooking – shrimp and scallops should only be added to the slow cooker during the last 30 to 60 minutes of cooking and cooking times for fish should be under 2 hours. If you do it right, using the slow cooker to cook your fish and seafood is a simple way to achieve moist, flavorful seafood dishes.

Shrimp Scampi

Traditionally, shrimp scampi is made with butter which gives it a high fat content and prevents it from fitting into the Paleolithic diet. By substituting ghee for the butter, however, you can still enjoy this flavorful dish while following the Paleo nutritional guidelines. This shrimp scampi makes a wonderful appetizer but you can also turn it into a meal by serving it on a bed of spaghetti squash or steamed veggies.

Number of Servings: 8   **Prep Time:** 10 Minutes

Ingredients:

2lb cooked shrimp
½ cup ghee
1 tbsp. olive oil
4 cloves garlic, minced
1 tbsp. fresh parsley, chopped
1 lemon, cut in half
Salt and pepper to taste

Instructions:

1. Combine the ghee, olive oil, garlic and parsley in the slow cooker.

2. Squeeze in the juice from the lemon and season with salt and pepper to taste.
3. Cover and cook on LOW heat for 5 to 6 hours.
4. Add the cooked shrimp to the slow cooker and cook on LOW heat for an additional fifteen minutes. Do not overcook.
5. Serve hot on a bed of spaghetti squash or steamed veggies.

Nutritional Information:

252 calories, 153 calories from fat, 24 g protein, 1 g carbohydrates, 17 g fat, 0 g sugar

Cooking Tips: If you prefer to purchase fresh shrimp rather than cooked shrimp you can easily cook it yourself at home before using it in this recipe. Simple heat some ghee or your preferred oil in a skillet over medium high heat then add the shrimp and cook for 2 to 3 minutes until evenly pink. Refrigerate the cooked shrimp until you are ready to use it.

Lemon Garlic Scallops

Scallops are a high-protein, low-calorie food that is full of flavor. Cooked in garlic and ghee, these scallops are rich and tender, perfectly seasoned with fresh parsley and a little lemon juice. This dish can be served over a bed of steamed vegetables or you can use it as an appetizer at your next dinner party. Simple arrange the scallops on a platter with some wooden toothpicks for your guests to use.

Number of Servings: 6   **Prep Time:** 15 Minutes

Ingredients:

2 lbs. bay scallops
3 tbsp. ghee
3 cloves garlic, sliced
1 lemon, thinly sliced
½ cup fresh parsley, chopped
Salt and pepper to taste
Lemon wedges

Instructions:

1. Rinse the scallops and pat them dry with a paper towel.
2. Add the ghee, garlic and lemon slices to the slow cooker.
3. Cover and cook on HIGH heat for 30 minutes or until the ghee is melted.

4. Add the scallops to the slow cooker and stir them into the ghee mixture. Season with salt and pepper to taste.
5. Cover again and cook on HIGH heat for 30 to 40 minutes or until scallops are cook through and tender.
6. Discard the lemon slices and serve the scallops with some of the cooking liquid.
7. Garnish with fresh parsley and lemon wedges.

Nutritional Information:

160 calories, 72 calories from fat, 20 g protein, 3 g carbohydrates, 8 g fat, 0 g sugar

Tangy Citrus Tilapia

Fresh fish is not only a great source of protein but it is also very easy to prepare, especially if you use your slow cooker. This recipe for tangy citrus tilapia is a light, summertime meal which can be customized with different citrus flavors depending what is in season. If seasoning the tilapia with citrus isn't enough for you, try making up a batch of citrus salsa to serve with your fish for a little extra flavor.

Number of Servings: **Prep Time:**

Ingredients:

1 ½ lbs. fresh tilapia fillets
1 small red onion, chopped
2 tsp. lemon zest
2 tsp. orange zest
5 tbsp. fresh parsley, chopped
1 tbsp. olive oil
Salt and pepper to taste

Instructions:

1. Coat the inside of your slow cooker with cooking spray.
2. Season the tilapia fillets with salt and pepper then place them in the slow cooker.
3. Add the onion, lemon zest, orange zest and fresh parsley.
4. Drizzle the olive oil over the ingredients in the slow cooker.

5. Cover and cook on LOW heat for 1 ½ hours.
6. Garnish with lemon slices and serve hot.

Nutritional Information:

calories, calories from fat, g protein, g carbohydrates, g fat, g sugar

Cooking Tips: To add some extra flavor to this recipe, serve your tilapia with fresh citrus salsa. Simply chop slices of orange, peach and mango then drizzle with fresh lemon juice and season with salt and fresh parsley to create a citrus salsa.

Salmon Sweet Potato Casserole

Casseroles are the perfect dish for potluck dinners and outdoor picnics because you do not need any special dishes to serve them – you can simply bring your slow cooker insert along. This recipe for salmon sweet potato casserole is not only easy to prepare, but it is something you have probably never tried before. The combination of seafood and sweet potatoes may seem strange, but there is something about these two flavors that blends perfectly to create a delicious, satisfying casserole.

Number of Servings: 6   **Prep Time:** 10 Minutes

Ingredients:

1lb salmon fillet, cooked
5 medium sweet potatoes
1 small onion, diced
3 tbsp. almond flour
6 eggs
¼ cup water
Salt and pepper to taste

Instructions:

1. Coat the inside of the slow cooker with cooking spray.
2. Peel and slice the sweet potatoes then layer half of them inside the slow cooker.

3. Season the sweet potatoes with salt and pepper then sprinkle on half the almond flour.
4. Break up the cooked salmon fillet with a fork and sprinkle half of it along with half the diced onion on top of the sweet potatoes in the slow cooker.
5. Repeat to create a second layer each of sweet potatoes then salmon and onions.
6. Beat the eggs with the water and pour over the ingredients in the slow cooker.
7. Cover and cook on LOW heat for 6 to 8 hours until sweet potatoes are tender.

Nutritional Information:
534 calories, 252 calories from fat, 46 g protein, 24 g carbohydrates, 28 g fat, 11 g sugar

Cooking Tips: To cook the salmon yourself, simply brush it with a little olive oil and place it on a baking tray in the oven at 350°F for 10 to 15 minutes. When the salmon is cooked, it should be moist and flakey.

Cioppino

Also called Fisherman's Stew, cioppino is a wonderful seafood dish that can actually be very easy to make if you use your slow cooker. Though this recipe calls for shrimp, scallops, mussels and cod you can feel free to add or substitute whatever type of seafood you prefer. Don't be afraid to add some fresh clams or to swap out a different type of fish fillet.

Number of Servings: 6   **Prep Time:** 15 Minutes

Ingredients:

½ lb. raw shrimp, peeled and deveined

½ lb. scallops, rinsed and patted dry

½ lb. mussels

½ lb. cod fillet, deboned and cubed

1 (28oz) can organic crushed tomatoes

1 cup tomato sauce

1 medium onion, chopped

3 cloves garlic, minced

1/3 cup olive oil

½ cup water

½ cup fresh parsley, chopped

1 tsp. thyme

1 tsp. oregano

Salt and pepper to taste

Instructions:

1. Place all the ingredients except for the seafood in the slow cooker.
2. Cover and cook on LOW heat for 6 to 8 hours.
3. Add the seafood to the slow cooker.
4. Cover and cook on HIGH for 30 minutes, stirring occasionally.

Nutritional Information:

258 calories, 117 calories from fat, 19 g protein, 16 g carbohydrates, 13 g fat, 6 g sugar

Shrimp Creole

Shrimp creole is a popular dish originating from New Orleans in Louisiana. A combination of French, African and Spanish flavors, this dish is certainly unique. If you love seafood and are looking for something out of the ordinary to serve at your next dinner party, consider this recipe for slow cooker Paleo shrimp creole. Not only is it incredibly flavorful, but it is also very easy to prepare.

Number of Servings: 4   **Prep Time:** 15 minutes

Ingredients:

1lb shrimp, peeled and deveined
1 green pepper, chopped
1 onion, chopped
2 stalks celery, diced
1 cup tomato sauce
3 cups tomatoes, chopped
2 cloves garlic, minced
¼ tsp. cayenne pepper
Salt and pepper to taste

Instructions:

1. Place all the ingredients in the slow cooker except for the shrimp.
2. Cover and cook on LOW heat for 6 to 8 hours or on HIGH heat for 3 to 4 hours.

3. Add the shrimp to the slow cooker for the last 30 minutes to 1 hour of cooking.
4. Garnish with sliced scallions and serve hot over a bed of steamed veggies or spaghetti squash.

Nutritional Information:
137 calories, 9 calories from fat, 17 g protein, 16 g carbohydrates, 1 g fat, 7 g sugar

Vegetarian Dishes

Whether you are cooking for vegetarian friends or are simply looking for a tasty, veggie-based recipe, these vegetarian dishes are sure to please. To make the most of these recipes, scout out your local farmers market or try growing some vegetables at home. This will ensure that the produce you use in these vegetarian dishes is fresh, thus ensuring that you get the best flavor. If you do not have access to fresh local produce, however, you can still find plenty of options in the organic section of your local grocery store.

Summer Squash Casserole

This recipe for summer squash casserole is the perfect way to use fresh zucchini and summer squash from your local farmers market. If you grow your own vegetables at home, it is also a great way to use the leftovers from your summer harvest. If you do not have any summer squash on hand you can easily substitute zucchini for the same effect.

Number of Servings: 4   **Prep Time:** 5 Minutes

Ingredients:

6 cups sliced yellow summer squash
1 small red onion, chopped
1 large carrot, peeled and shredded
¼ cup almond flour
1 cup vegetable stock
¼ cup ghee

Instructions:

1. Combine the vegetables in a large bowl, mixing to combine, then add them to the slow cooker.
2. Whisk together the flour and vegetable stock.
3. Pour the vegetable stock over the vegetables in the slow cooker and dot with pats of ghee.
4. Cover and cook on LOW heat for 6 to 8 hours until the squash in tender.

Nutritional Information:

204 calories, 162 calories from fat, 4 g protein, 10 g carbohydrates, 18 g fat, 6 g sugar

Cooking Tips: If you don't have any yellow summer squash on hand you can easily substitute zucchini in this recipe. You may even want to use a mixture of the two if you have them both.

Eggplant Parmesan

Eggplant parmesan is a vegetarian-friendly alternative to the traditional Italian dish chicken parmesan. When made with fresh eggplant, this dish is incredibly flavorful and, with the help of your slow cooker, it is also easy to prepare. While many people who follow the Paleolithic diet completely omit dairy, vegetarians often choose to include some dairy to ensure that their nutritional needs are met. If you do choose to eat dairy, feel free to sprinkle some mozzarella cheese on top of your eggplant parmesan.

Number of Servings: 6   **Prep Time:** 20 Minutes

Ingredients:

4 medium eggplants, peeled
2 eggs
3 tbsp. almond flour
1/3 cup water
2 tsp. olive oil
3 cups organic tomato sauce

Instructions:

1. Cut the eggplant lengthwise into ½-inch slices. Drain the slices on pieces of paper towel.
2. Combine the eggs, water and almond flour to form a batter.
3. Heat the olive oil in a large skillet over medium heat.

4. Drip the eggplant slices into the batter then place them in the hot skillet. Sauté the eggplant for 30 seconds to one minute on each side.
5. Layer the sautéed eggplant in the bottom of the slow cooker. Make a second layer of slices, arranging them so they face in the opposite direction. Repeat until all the eggplant is used.
6. Pour the tomato sauce into the slow cooker.
7. Cover and cook on LOW heat for 4 to 5 hours.

Nutritional Information:

197 calories, 54 calories from fat, 7g protein, 34 g carbohydrates, 6 g fat, 11 g sugar

Spaghetti Squash

When cooked properly, spaghetti squash looks just like what it is named after – spaghetti. This squash is incredibly easy to cook and it is very versatile. If you season it well, you can enjoy this food as a main course or you can use it to form a bed for steamed veggies, stew or other foods.

Number of Servings: 4   **Prep Time:** 5 Minutes

Ingredients:

1 spaghetti squash
2 cups water

Instructions:

1. Use a sharp knife or fork to puncture the spaghetti squash several times.
2. Place the squash in the slow cooker then pour in the water.
3. Cover and cook on LOW heat for 8 to 9 hours.
4. Remove the squash from the slow cooker then cut in half and remove the seeds. Use a fork to separate the squash from the rind into a bowl.
5. Season as desired and serve hot.

Nutritional Information:
23 calories, 0 calories from fat, 0 g protein, 5 g carbohydrates, 0 g fat, 0 g sugar

Tomato Spinach Soup

If you are looking for a light meal, this recipe is a delicious twist on traditional tomato soup. The addition of spinach to the recipe gives this soup an interesting flavor while also adding a few more healthy nutrients. Don't be afraid to try out this recipe on your family and friends – even non-vegetarians are sure to enjoy it.

Number of Servings: 6   **Prep Time:** 10 Minutes

Ingredients:

12 oz. baby spinach, rinsed
1 can roasted diced tomatoes
2 stalks celery, sliced
2 carrots, sliced
1 onion, chopped
2 cloves garlic, minced
4 cups organic vegetable broth
¼ cup fresh basil, chopped
1 tsp. dried oregano
Salt and pepper to taste

Instructions:

1. Combine the vegetables in the slow cooker then add the garlic.

2. Stir together the vegetable broth, basil, oregano, salt and pepper then pour it into the slow cooker.
3. Cover and cook on LOW heat for 8 to 10 hours or HIGH heat for 4 to 6 hours.
4. Garnish with additional basil leaves and serve hot.

Nutritional Information:

62 calories, 0 calories from fat, 3 g protein, 12 g carbohydrates, 0 g fat, 5 g sugar

Winter Vegetable Stew

A vegetable stew is the perfect meal for a cold winter evening – the delicious combination of steamy vegetable broth and tender winter vegetables is sure to fill you up and warm your belly. The best part about this recipe is that you can easily customize it according to what vegetables you have available. Feel free to substitute sweet potatoes for the red gold potatoes, add more carrots or omit an ingredient you don't like.

Number of Servings: 8   **Prep Time:** 15 Minutes

Ingredients:

4 red potatoes, diced
3 large carrots, sliced
3 large stalks celery, sliced
2 parsnips, peeled and diced
2 leeks, diced (white and green parts only)
2 cans organic diced tomatoes
2 cups organic vegetable broth
1 sprig fresh rosemary
2 bay leaves
Salt and pepper to taste

Instructions:

1. Combine the first six ingredients in the slow cooker.
2. Pour the vegetable broth over the vegetables in the slow cooker then add the rosemary and bay leaves.
3. Season with salt and pepper to taste.
4. Cover and cook on LOW heat for 8 to 10 hours until vegetables are tender.
5. Remove rosemary and bay leaves before serving.

Nutritional Information:

155 calories, 9 calories from fat, 4 g protein, 35 g carbohydrates, 1 g fat, 9 g sugar

Snacks and Appetizers

If you are in need of a few recipes for quick and tasty snacks and appetizers, these slow cooker Paleo recipes may be just what you are looking for. From tangy mini meatballs to zucchini bread and applesauce, these snacks and appetizers are more than just delicious – they are healthy too! Whether you are cooking for a dinner party or for your family at home, these recipes will satisfy cravings and fill hungry bellies without you having to slave over the stove for several hours. By using your slow cooker, you need only spend a few minutes preparing these dishes then you can walk away for a few hours while they cook. When you return, you will find that your slow cooker has done most of the work for you and your tasty snacks and appetizers are ready to serve!

Mini Meatballs

Though simple to prepare, these mini meatballs are full of flavor and sure to be a hit at your next dinner party. The combination of tomato sauce and honey creates a light, sweet flavor that cooks into the meatballs, leaving them tender and juicy. If you are feeling adventurous, feel free to experiment a little bit to create your own sauce for mini meatballs. Try adding some cayenne to spice things up or omit the honey in place of some marinara sauce for a more traditional side dish of meatballs and tomato sauce.

Number of Servings: 5   **Prep Time:** 15 minutes

Ingredients:

1lb grass-fed ground beef
1 onion, diced
1 tsp. salt
¼ tsp. pepper
1 clove garlic, minced
2 tbsp. coconut oil
1 (15 oz.) can organic tomato sauce
2 tbsp. organic honey

Instructions:

1. Combine the beef, onion, salt, pepper and garlic in a bowl and mix well. Shape the beef into mini meatballs and set aside.

2. Heat the coconut oil in a skillet over medium high heat. Add the meatballs and cook them for 5 minutes or until brown on all sides.
3. Place the meatballs in the slow cooker.
4. Whisk together the tomato sauce and honey then pour over the meatballs.
5. Cover and cook on LOW heat for 3 to 4 hours or until meatballs are cooked through.

Nutritional Information:

292 calories, 135 calories from fat, 23 g protein, 16 g carbohydrates, 15 g fat, 9 g sugar

Creamy Artichoke Dip

Number of Servings: 4   **Prep Time:** 10 Minutes

Ingredients:

1 ripe avocado
1 (6 oz.) jar artichoke hearts
2 small zucchini, peeled and diced
½ large lemon
2 cloves garlic, peeled
1 tbsp. olive oil
Salt and pepper to taste

Instructions:

1. Combine the avocado, artichoke hearts, zucchini and garlic in a food processor. Pulse to blend until well combined.
2. Pour the mixture into the slow cooker and squeeze the lemon over it.
3. Drizzle the olive oil around the outer edges of the slow cooker and season to taste with salt and pepper.
4. Cover and cook on LOW heat for 3 hours.
5. Serve hot with fresh vegetables for dipping.

Nutritional Information:

141 calories, 99 calories from fat, 3 g protein, 10 g carbohydrates, 11 g fat, 3 g sugar

Zucchini Bread

Number of Servings: 10   **Prep Time:** 20 Minutes

Ingredients:

2 cups zucchini, shredded
1 ½ cups almond flour
2 eggs
¾ cup honey
¼ cup coconut oil
½ tsp. salt
½ tsp. baking soda
1/8 tsp. baking powder
1 ½ tsp. ground cinnamon
1 ½ tsp. vanilla extract
½ cup chopped walnuts

Instructions:

1. Sift together the salt, baking soda, baking powder, ground cinnamon and almond flour into a medium bowl. Set aside.
2. Combine the eggs, honey, coconut oil and vanilla extract until well blended. Stir in the dry ingredients until a moist batter forms.

3. Fold in the shredded zucchini and chopped walnut.
4. Coat the inside of a slow cooker insert pan with cooking spray and pour in the batter.
5. Cover and cook on HIGH heat for 2 to 3 hours. Cool slightly before serving.

Nutritional Information:

283 calories, 171 calories from fat, 7 g protein, 27 g carbohydrates,19 g fat, 22 g sugar

Applesauce

Number of Servings: 10   **Prep Time:** 10 Minutes

Ingredients:

8 large apples, peeled and chopped
½ jar container apple juice concentrate
Ground cinnamon

Instructions:

1. Place the apple chunks in the slow cooker and add the apple juice concentrate.
2. Cover and cook on LOW heat for 4 to 6 hours until the apples are tender, stirring every hour.
3. Turn off the slow cooker and puree in a blender or use an immersion blender.
4. Stir in ground cinnamon to taste.

Nutritional Information:

123 calories, 0 calories from fat, 0 g protein, 31 g carbohydrates, 0 g fat, 27 g sugar

Red Pepper Dip

Number of Servings: 4   **Prep Time:** 5 Minutes

Ingredients:

4 red peppers, cored
1 small onion, sliced thin
2 garlic cloves, minced
2 tsp. olive oil
Salt and pepper to taste

Instructions:

1. Core and dice the red peppers.
2. Place the red peppers, onions and garlic in a food processor. Drizzle with one teaspoon of olive oil then pulse to puree.
3. Pour the puree into the slow cooker and drizzle with remaining olive oil. Season with salt and pepper to taste.
4. Cover and cook on LOW heat for 3 hours.
5. Cool slightly before serving with sliced veggies for dipping.

Nutritional Information:
64 calories, 27 calories from fat, 1 g protein, g carbohydrates, 3 g fat, 4 g sugar

Cooking Tips: To add some more flavor to this recipe, try turning it into a roasted red pepper dip. After coring your red peppers, cut them in half and lay them face down on a hot grill for a minute or two to char the edges. After charring the peppers, simply chop them up and continue with the rest of the recipe as written.

Side Dishes

Whether you are looking for something to accompany your next family dinner or you are in need of a dish to take to a church potluck or family picnic, these slow cooker Paleo recipes for side dishes are perfect. From casseroles to stuffed peppers, these recipes are both unique and delicious. The best part about these recipes is that, in most cases, the ingredients are interchangeable – if you do not have zucchini on hand, for example, you can substitute another type of in-season squash. Not only are these recipes easy and healthy, but they are a great way to use up the leftovers from your vegetable garden harvest. If you do not grow your own vegetables at home, check out your local farmer's market to find some fresh produce.

Sweet Potato Casserole

This recipe for sweet potato casserole is the perfect way to serve sweet potatoes. With only a few minutes of preparation required, you will have a hot, delicious bowl full of tender sweet potatoes. Try out this recipe at your next family dinner or save it for a special occasion like Thanksgiving. Do not be afraid to experiment, either – try adding some chopped nuts or dried fruit for extra flavor!

Number of Servings: 6   **Prep Time:** 10 Minutes

Ingredients:

6 sweet potatoes, peeled and sliced
2 medium onions, diced
8 eggs
½ tsp. paprika
Salt and pepper to taste

Instructions:

1. Coat the inside of your slow cooker with cooking spray.
2. Peel the sweet potatoes and slice them into 1/8th inch slices then line the bottom of your slow cooker with the slices. Create as many layers as you need, alternating the direction of the slices on each layer.
3. Beat the eggs together with the paprika, salt and pepper in a medium bowl.
4. Pour the egg mixture into the slow cooker.

5. Cover and cook on LOW heat for 5 to 6 hours or until the sweet potatoes are tender.
6. Turn off the slow cooker and cool for 30 minutes before serving.

Nutritional Information:

225 calories, 63 calories from fat, 11 g protein, 30 g carbohydrates, 7 g fat, 8 g sugar

Cooking Tips: If you want to sweeten your casserole, feel free to drizzle some organic honey over each layer of sweet potato slices. You can also consider adding some raisins or another dried fruit to the mixture in the slow cooker.

Zucchini Casserole

Growing your own produce can be a wonderful experience and an inexpensive way to get fresh, organic produce. If you are not careful, however, you may end up with an abundance of produce that you do not know what to do with. If you have found yourself in this boat with your zucchini plants, this recipe for zucchini casserole is the perfect solution. Serve up this dish with dinner at home or bring it to your next potluck dinner.

Number of Servings: 10   **Prep Time:** 15 Minutes

Ingredients:

2 medium zucchinis, sliced
2 medium yellow squash, sliced
1 medium red onion, sliced
1 red pepper, julienned
1 lb. tomatoes, diced
1 tsp. salt
½ tsp. pepper
1 tbsp. coconut oil

Instructions:

1. Combine the zucchini, squash, onion, peppers and tomatoes in the slow cooker.
2. Sprinkle with salt and pepper.
3. Cover and cook on LOW heat for 3 hours.

4. Remove the lid and drizzle the coconut oil on top of the vegetables in the slow cooker.
5. Cover again and cook on LOW for an additional hour.

Nutritional Information:

45 calories, 18 calories from fat, 2g protein, 7 g carbohydrates, 2 g fat, 4 g sugar

Stuffed Peppers

Though often served as an entrée, stuffed peppers also make a wonderful side dish for dinner parties and potluck dinners. To truly make this dish a side dish rather than an entrée, use small bell peppers rather than large ones. If you grow your own peppers at home, pick the peppers when they reach about 3 inches in diameter.

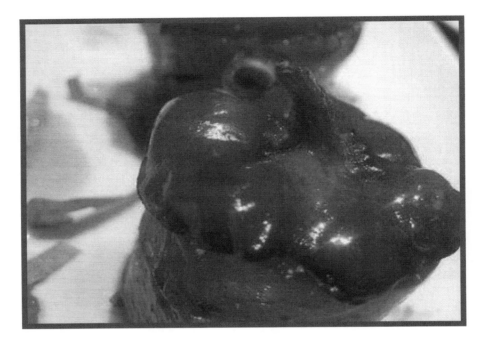

Number of Servings: 6   **Prep Time:** 10 Minutes

Ingredients:

8 small bell peppers, any color
½ head cauliflower
½ lb. grass-fed ground beef
½ lb. lean ground turkey
1 onion, diced
3 cloves garlic, minced
1 (6 oz.) can tomato paste
¼ cup water
1 tbsp. Italian seasoning
Salt and pepper to taste

Instructions:

1. Cut the cauliflower into florets and pulse it in a food processor along with the onions and garlic.

2. Slice the tops off the peppers and remove the seeds, preserving the top of the pepper.
3. Combine the pulsed vegetables with the ground meat, tomato paste, Italian seasoning, salt and pepper in a medium bowl.
4. Stuff the meat mixture into the peppers and replace the tops.
5. Arrange the stuffed peppers in the slow cooker and pour the water into the slow cooker around them.
6. Cover and cook on LOW heat for 6 to 8 hours.

Nutritional Information:

189 calories, 45 calories from fat, 20 g protein, 9 g carbohydrates, 5 g fat, 5 g sugar

Lemon Brussels Sprouts

Brussels sprouts are an underappreciated vegetable but, when cooked properly, they can be quite delicious. This recipe for lemon Brussels sprouts yields four servings of tender, flavorful Brussels sprouts that make a wonderful side dish for virtually any meal. After trying this recipe once you may find that you like it so much you turn it into a meal on its own!

Number of Servings: 4   **Prep Time:** 10 Minutes

Ingredients:

2 lbs. Brussels sprouts
1 red onion, diced
3 small lemons
3 tbsp. coconut oil
Salt and pepper to taste
1/2 cup water

Instructions:

1. Wash the Brussels sprouts then trim off the ends and cut them in half. Place them in the slow cooker.
2. Add the diced onions to the slow cooker, stirring them into the Brussels sprouts.
3. Drizzle the coconut oil over top of the ingredients in the slow cooker and season with salt and pepper to taste.
4. Squeeze the lemons over the ingredients in the slow cooker then stir to evenly distribute the juice.

5. Pour in ½ cup water then cover and cook on LOW heat for 4 to 5 hours or on HIGH heat for 2 to 3 hours.

Nutritional Information:

185 calories, 99 calories from fat, 9 g protein, g carbohydrates, 11 g fat, 4 g sugar

Glazed Carrots

These carrots are subtly sweetened with honey which helps to bring out the natural flavor of these fresh, wonderful vegetables. If you have picky eaters in your household who do not like to eat their vegetables, these glazed carrots may be enough to tempt them. Not only are these carrots incredibly flavorful, but they are also very easy to prepare.

Number of Servings: 6   **Prep Time:** 10 Minutes

Ingredients:

2 lb. baby carrots
¼ cup organic honey
1 ½ cups water
2 tbsp. coconut butter
Salt and pepper to taste

Instructions:

1. Place the carrots in the slow cooker and cover with water.
2. Cover and cook on LOW heat for 6 to 8 hours or until the carrots are tender.
3. Drain the water from the slow cooker and stir in the honey, coconut butter, salt and pepper.
4. Cover again and cook on LOW heat for 30 minutes until the honey melts into a glaze.

Nutritional Information:
133 calories, 27 calories from fat, 2 g protein, 27 g carbohydrates, 3 g fat, 20 g sugar

Desserts

Many people assume that when you start following a more healthy diet that you have to give up desserts. While it is true that you should limit your intake of sweet, high-calorie foods like desserts, you do not need to give them up entirely. There are plenty of ways to stick to your Paleolithic diet while also enjoying the occasional sweet treat. Rather than reaching for a candy bar or a scoop of ice cream, think about trying some of these fruit-based recipes. Fruit is naturally sweet and contains a variety of healthy nutrients that your body needs. It may be hard to believe but sometimes dessert can actually be good for you!

Dark Chocolate Brownies

No matter what type of diet you are on, you should still be able to enjoy the occasional treat. The key to sticking to the rules of the Paleolithic diet while still enjoying the occasional dessert is to avoid refine sugars – use some type of natural sweetener like honey or agave nectar as a substitute.

Number of Servings: 14   **Prep Time:** 20 Minutes

Ingredients:

½ cup unsweetened baking cocoa

1 ½ cups almond flour

8 oz. unsweetened dark chocolate, chopped

4 tbsp. coconut butter

3 eggs, beaten

1 cup honey

1 tbsp. vanilla extract

3/4 tsp. baking soda

1/2 tsp. salt

1 cup walnuts, chopped

Instructions:

1. Coat the inside of your slow cooker with cooking spray then line the bottom with parchment paper to make it easier to remove the brownies.
2. Combine the almond flour, cocoa powder, baking powder and salt in a small bowl. Set aside.

106

3. Heat the unsweetened dark chocolate, honey and coconut butter in a double boiler over medium heat. Stir often until the chocolate is melted and the mixture is smooth.
4. Remove from heat and stir in the eggs. Stir in the flour mixture then fold in the walnuts. Do not over-stir.
5. Pour the batter into the slow cooker and spread it evenly.
6. Cover and cook on LOW heat for 3 ½ hours. Uncover and cook for an additional 30 minutes to create a crust on top of the brownies.
7. Cool completely before removing from the slow cooker to cut and serve.

Nutritional Information:
330 calories, 216 calories from fat, 9 g protein, 31 g carbohydrates,24 g fat, 21 g sugar

Pumpkin Pie Pudding

If you are in the mood for pumpkin pie but do not want to go through the hassle of making up a pie crust – or if you have decided to completely omit grains and flours from your diet – this recipe is the perfect solution. This slow cooker Paleo recipe for pumpkin pie pudding is the perfect way to enjoy a fall favorite while still sticking to your Paleolithic diet.

Number of Servings: 8   **Prep Time:** 20 Minutes

Ingredients:

1 (15oz) can pumpkin puree
¼ cup coconut milk
¼ cup honey
1 cup toasted pecans, chopped
1 cup almond flour
2 tbsp. pumpkin pie spice
¼ cup coconut butter, melted

Instructions:

1. Coat the inside of the slow cooker with cooking spray.
2. Combine the pumpkin puree, coconut milk, honey and half of the pumpkin pie spice in a medium bowl, stirring to combine. Add the batter to the slow cooker.

3. Stir together the almond flour, pecans and remaining pumpkin pie spice in another bowl then sprinkle it over top of the batter in the slow cooker.
4. Drizzle the melted coconut butter over the ingredients in the slow cooker.
5. Cover and cook on HIGH heat for 2 ½ hours. Turn off the slow cooker and cool for 30 minutes before serving.

Nutritional Information:

268 calories, 198 calories from fat, 6 g protein, 19 g carbohydrates, 22 g fat, 11 g sugar

Raisin-Stuffed Apples

If you want to enjoy the flavor of decadent apple pie while still sticking to the principles of the Paleolithic diet, this recipe is perfect for you. These raisin-stuffed apples are a snap to prepare and as they cook in your slow cooker they will fill your home with the delicious aroma of apple and cinnamon. Once you try this recipe feel free to experiment with different substitutions to achieve different flavors – try adding some chopped nuts or swap out the raisins for another type of dried fruit.

Number of Servings: 4   **Prep Time:** 20 Minutes

Ingredients:

4 tart apples (Granny Smith)
1/3 cup raisins
¼ cup honey
½ tsp. ground cinnamon
¼ cup organic apple juice
1 tbsp. ghee

Instructions:

1. Core the apples and place them upright in the bottom of your slow cooker.
2. Combine the raisins, honey and cinnamon in a small bowl then spoon the mixture into the apples.
3. Pour the apple juice into the slow cooker around the apples and top each apple with a small dollop of ghee.

4. Cover and cook on LOW heat for 5 hours or on HIGH heat for 2 ½ hours.
5. Use a slotted spoon to remove the apples from the slow cooker and serve hot.

Nutritional Information:

226 calories, 36 calories from fat, 0 g protein, 52 g carbohydrates, 4 g fat, 46 g sugar

Peach Blackberry Fruit Crisp

Whether you are looking for a sweet summertime dessert or something to bring to a company picnic, this recipe for peach blackberry fruit crisp is perfect. Not only can you customize this recipe to utilize different fruit combinations, but you can also double or triple the recipe very easily to serve a large number of people. Make the most of the summer months by using recipes like this one to enjoy fresh fruit while it is in season.

Number of Servings: 6   **Prep Time:** 10 Minutes

Ingredients:

1lb fresh peaches, sliced
1 pint fresh blackberries
1 ½ cups almond meal
2 tbsp. coconut butter
1 tsp. ground cinnamon
Drizzle organic honey

Instructions:

1. Coat the inside of the slow cooker with cooking spray.
2. Combine the sliced peaches and blackberries in the slow cooker.
3. Pour the almond meal and ground cinnamon into a medium bowl, stirring to combine. Cut in the coconut butter using a pastry cutter.

4. Sprinkle the almond meal mixture on top of the fruit in the slow cooker and drizzle with organic honey.
5. Cover and heat on LOW for 2 ½ hours.
6. Turn off the slow cooker and cool for 30 minutes before serving.

Nutritional Information:

250 calories, 153 calories from fat, 8 g protein, 22 g carbohydrates, 17 g fat, 12 g sugar

Cooking Tips: This recipe is the perfect summertime dessert because you can customize it using whatever fruit is in season. If you happen to grow your own fruit or have access to fresh local produce, don't be afraid to try out a variety of combinations. You be surprised at what you can come up with!

Spiced Fruit Compote

Spiced fruit compote is a light, healthy dessert that is sure to satisfy your sweet tooth. Rather than relying on refined sugars for its sweetness, however, this recipe plays up the natural sweetness of fresh fruit and berries like pears, strawberries, pineapple and cherries. If you don't have one of these fruits on hand, feel free to substitute another type of fresh in-season fruit.

Number of Servings: 10   **Prep Time:** 15 Minutes

Ingredients:

3 fresh pears, cored and cubed

1 cup strawberries, sliced

1 cups pineapple, cubed

1 cup dried apricots, chopped

2 cups pitted cherries

3 tbsp. orange juice concentrate

2 tbsp. organic honey

½ tsp. ground ginger

1 cup chopped walnuts

Instructions:

1. Combine the pears, strawberries, pineapple, apricots and cherries in the slow cooker.
2. Stir together the honey, orange juice concentrate and ground ginger then stir it into the ingredients in the slow cooker.

3. Sprinkle the chopped nuts on top then cover and cook on LOW heat for 6 to 8 hours or on HIGH for 3 to 4 hours.

4. Turn off the slow cooker and cool for 30 minutes before spooning into dishes to serve.

Nutritional Information:

197 calories, 72 calories from fat, 3 g protein, 33 g carbohydrates, 8 g fat, 22 g sugar

Image Credits

Cover Photo, page 1, Flickr user Thepinkpeppercorn,
<http://www.flickr.com/photos/gail_thepinkpeppercorn/4994405811/>

Introduction Photo, Page 2, By Takeaway (Own work) [CC-BY-SA-3.0
(http://creativecommons.org/licenses/by-sa/3.0)], via Wikimedia Commons

Peanut Chicken Soup, Page 7, Flickr user KayOne73,
<http://www.flickr.com/photos/kayone73/5941715023/>

Roasted Leek, Potato and Onion Soup, Flickr user Ned Raggett,
<http://www.flickr.com/photos/nedraggett/264536172/>

Chicken and Sweet Potato Stew, Flickr user Jeffreyw,
<http://www.flickr.com/photos/jeffreyww/5058084454/>

Tomato Basil Soup, Flickr user Lara604, <http://www.flickr.com/photos/lara604/4104748556/>

Greek Stew, Flickr user Avlxyz, <http://www.flickr.com/photos/avlxyz/1221497455/>

Jambalaya, Flickr user Swift Benjamin, <http://www.flickr.com/photos/metalcowboy/407484130/>

Butternut Squash Soup, Flickr user Ross Catrow,
<http://www.flickr.com/photos/maxpower/4154866746/>

Thai Curry Chicken Soup, Flickr user Alvxyz, <http://www.flickr.com/photos/avlxyz/4159582624/>

Lemon Garlic Chicken, Flickr user Ralph and Jenny,
<http://www.flickr.com/photos/ralphandjenny/2847861383/>

Chicken and Gravy, Flickr user Sifu Renka, <http://www.flickr.com/photos/sifu_renka/3335233773/>

Lettuce Wrapped Chicken, Flickr user BrownGuacamole,
<http://farm3.staticflickr.com/2268/2287264841_75d9f4100f.jpg>

Teriyaki Chicken Drumsticks, Flickr user TheCulinaryGeek,
<http://www.flickr.com/photos/preppybyday/4777525079/>

Asparagus Chicken Roll-Ups, Flickr user Slopjop, <http://www.flickr.com/photos/slopjop/2747466571/>

Spicy Pulled Chicken, Flickr user MallyDally,
<http://www.flickr.com/photos/39975765@N05/6620178655/>

Chicken and Cabbage, Flickr user Balise42, <http://www.flickr.com/photos/ipalatin/5426338736/>

Chicken Cacciatore, Flickr user TheCulinaryGeek,
  <http://www.flickr.com/photos/preppybyday/4618397089/>

Raw Chicken, page 23, By Dnor (Own work) [Public domain], via Wikimedia Commons

BBQ Short Ribs, Flickr user WordRidden, <http://www.flickr.com/photos/wordridden/4897726842/>

Spicy Beef Stew, Flickr user Pellesten, <http://www.flickr.com/photos/pellesten/5550912116/>

Sweet Balsamic Roast Beef, Flickr user Candyschwartz, <http://www.flickr.com/photos/candy-s/5315649359/>

Meatloaf, Flickr user NourishingCook, <http://www.flickr.com/photos/nourishingcook/5650744098/>

Beef with Broccoli, Flickr user Goodiesfirst, <http://www.flickr.com/photos/scaredykat/2926129514/>

Easy Lamb Roast, Flickr user Avlxyz, <http://www.flickr.com/photos/avlxyz/1654450159/>

Lamb Curry, Flickr user Special*Dark, <http://www.flickr.com/photos/allthingschill/2438560451/>

Lamb Stew, Flickr user Jeffreyw, <http://www.flickr.com/photos/jeffreyww/4568014155/>

Dried Apricot Lamb Casserole, Flickr user Itinerant Tightwad,
  <http://www.flickr.com/photos/itineranttightwad/3694711587/>

Osso Buco with Garlic Marinara, Flickr user Naotakem,
  <http://www.flickr.com/photos/naotakem/4694647019/>

Shrimp Scampi, Flickr user Startcooking, <http://www.flickr.com/photos/startcooking/2760564944/>

Lemon Garlic Scallops, Flickr user Jordanmit09,
  <http://www.flickr.com/photos/jordansorensen/3770624073/>

Tangy Citrus Tilapia, Flickr user Mallydally,
  <http://www.flickr.com/photos/39975765@N05/5972651530/>

Salmon Sweet Potato Casserole, Flickr user Karenandbrademerson,
  <http://www.flickr.com/photos/karenandbrademerson/3419998080/>

Cioppino, Flickr user Neeta Lind, <http://www.flickr.com/photos/neeta_lind/933329856/>

Shrimp Creole, Flickr user Gromgull, <http://www.flickr.com/photos/gromgull/2520856387/>

Summer Squash Casserole, Flickr user Dawn Gagnon,
<http://www.flickr.com/photos/dawnella66/6944312421/>

Eggplant Parmesan, Flickr user Adactio, <http://www.flickr.com/photos/adactio/1094959940/>

Spaghetti Squash, Flickr user @Bastique, <http://www.flickr.com/photos/bastique/6161415108/>

Spinach and Tomato Soup, Flickr user Wonderyort,
<http://www.flickr.com/photos/sharontroy/7343976732/>

Winter Vegetable Stew, Flickr user

Mini Meatballs, Flickr user Maggie Hoffman,
<http://www.flickr.com/photos/maggiejane/3237536211/>

Creamy Artichoke Dip, Flickr user Dave_Murr,   <http://www.flickr.com/photos/davemurr/7218227576/>

Zucchini Bread, Flickr user Ccharmon, <http://www.flickr.com/photos/9439733@N02/2157411940/>

Applesauce, Flickr user Lydiajoy1, <http://www.flickr.com/photos/51560758@N05/4949957840/>

Red Pepper Dip, Flickr user Veganheathen,
<http://www.flickr.com/photos/veganheathen/2115594149/>

Sweet Potato Casserole, Flickr user Rooey, < http://www.flickr.com/photos/rooey/5634374827/>

Zucchini Casserole, Flickr user YoAmes, <http://www.flickr.com/photos/24013072@N05/4199096836/>

Stuffed Peppers, Flickr user Annie Mole, <http://www.flickr.com/photos/anniemole/3963259894/>

Lemon Brussels Sprouts, Flickr user Mkosut, <http://www.flickr.com/photos/mkosut/3633458939/>

Glazed Carrots, Flickr user TinyRedKitchen,
<http://www.flickr.com/photos/62454420@N07/6583013659/>

Dark Chocolate Brownies, Flickr user JeffreyW, <http://www.flickr.com/photos/jeffreyww/4448807631/>

Pumpkin Pie Pudding, Flickr user Www.WorththeWisk.com,
<http://www.flickr.com/photos/27836576@N02/4029828855/>

Raisin-Stuffed Apples, Flickr user SleepyNeko, <http://www.flickr.com/photos/ejchang/365298820/>

Peach Blackberry Fruit Crisp, Flickr user Saucy Salad,
<http://www.flickr.com/photos/saucysalad/4902471974/>

Spiced Berry Compote, Flicker user Jojomzz, <http://www.flickr.com/photos/souschef/465114075/>

Printed in Great Britain
by Amazon.co.uk, Ltd.,
Marston Gate.